Time Management Strategies for Entrepreneurs

Other Titles By The Authors

The Inner Game of Internet Marketing

Huge Profits With a Tiny List

Weeping Willow: Volume One: Welcome to River Bend

Huge Profits With Affiliate Marketing

And many more...

Time Management Strategies For Entrepreneurs:

How To Manage Your Time To Increase Your Bottom Line

By

Connie Ragen Green
and Geoff Hoff

Copyright © 2013 by Hunter's Moon Publishing

978-1-937988-07-4

 Hunter's Moon Publishing

Dedication

This book is dedicated to people everywhere, especially entrepreneurs, who are struggling to find the time to do everything their hearts desire. Know that time is on your side, and that you can learn the skills necessary to manage your time and make it your ally as you live your mission and vision in your personal life and in your business.

Table of Contents

Introduction

When we made the decision to write this book on time management and productivity, we did so very quickly. Since coming online in 2006 it has been brought to Connie's attention many times that she is someone who makes excellent use of her time and resources on a daily basis. This includes making decisions almost immediately, taking action on tasks and activities that will move her closer to her goals, and saying no to opportunities that are actually obstacles to what she wishes to achieve. Geoff is someone who has had more recent struggles with time management, and we thought combining our two distinct experiences and the techniques we now use could be a powerful way to bring the topic home for people.

In her previous life as a classroom teacher for twenty years and a real estate appraiser and listing broker for longer than that, however, Connie did not feel like she had a grasp on these aspects of her life. Her days were long and filled with missed opportunities, exhaustion, and wasted time. On many occasions, she remembers thinking, 'where did the time go?' but had no answers. Here she was, teaching students to become organized, responsible, and productive adults, and having difficulty with these concepts herself. She started reading and listening to audio recordings to find the answers to her questions, and finally realized that taking a passive role in her own personal growth and development would not be enough. Instead, she changed her life completely by changing her thinking and becoming an active participant in her own progress. Slowly her life began to turn around, culminating in the decision to resign from the school district and to give away all of her real estate clients in order to become an online entrepreneur.

Geoff's journey was a bit different. In school, he always waited until the last possible moment to do any assignment, to start any homework, to even begin to read a book for a book report. Somehow, the stress and pressure of that usually got him moving, and he did well in school, but had he learned to manage his time way back then, his life would have been completely different. He took that habit well into his adult life. He learned that, when that pressure, that stress, mounted, it was time for a flurry of activity and the task would be completed. Stuff got done, but it took a huge toll on the way he lived his life. And there were projects that could have been glorious that never even got started, because he never got to that moment of do-or-die with them.

What he has noticed over the years, however, was that there were times when he had a firm grasp on what needed to be done and how best to do it in the time he had. These were usually when he was working on a project that involved more than just himself, a project that he was managing and one in which many people relied on him. Some of these projects were theatre projects, where he effectively managed a group of chaotic artistic types with the common goal of being absolutely ready for opening night. Some involved projects he managed for various work places, such as organizing the changeover from electric typewriters to computers in a law office, and later, getting all those computers networked together.

When he noticed that he had moments in his life when he was very good at managing his time and his productivity, he started looking at what was distinct in those moments that was missing from the other times in his life when he waited until the last possible moment to begin a task, when he waited for and relied on that familiar pressure to get things done. Much of what he discovered in that exploration will be shared in this book.

Now that Connie has transformed her life and taken charge of her own destiny, she has time to travel, volunteer with several non-profit and service organizations, author books, speak around the world, and daydream, along with having the skill and desire to run a highly successful and profitable business that brings her the joy and satisfaction that comes from helping others to achieve their own dreams and goals. And now that Geoff has begun to pull the lessons from the more productive times in his life into a strategy for everyday living, his business has taken off. But he isn't the only one to benefit. His clients and students also get great benefit.

Clearly, something inside of both Connie and Geoff has shifted since they made these decisions, Connie to leave that old life behind and become an entrepreneur, Geoff to examine what really worked in his own life. You can make these same changes, or ones that suit your lifestyle even more, by simply taking action with the information we are sharing in this book. Since everything in business consists of what are known as 'learnable skills', we are thrilled to pass this information on to you.

This is just part of what you will learn in this book. we will be sharing strategies and techniques based on our experiences and results throughout our entire adult lives, including those that have made a significant difference in our lives as well as what has not worked very well at all. If you are feeling pressed for time and overwhelmed, we have been there. If you know that you would be more energetic, more pleasant to be around, and financially better off if you could just manage your time for optimal productivity, we know what that's like as well and will address exactly how you can make these changes in your life, quickly and permanently. And, finally, if indecision has kept you from realizing your hopes and dreams in all areas of your life, we have been there as well and will guide you towards a simple way to make the right decisions in your life.

Be sure to read this book all the way through to learn how this process works. Then, go back and reread the sections that relate to what you need in your life right now. Rest assured that you will get what you need in order to become a more productive entrepreneur who will enjoy each day to the greatest extent possible.

Connie Ragen Green and Geoff Hoff
Los Angeles, 2012

Section I: Why Is Time Management So Important For Entrepreneurs?

"One of the differences between successful people and average people is how they value and manage their time. Ask yourself, 'what is the most valuable use of my time, right now', and work on that activity right away until it is completed."
~Brian Tracy

Before you can move forward with the ideas, concepts, and beliefs we will be explaining and sharing in this book, you must come to the conclusion that time management is indeed a worthwhile pursuit that will help you to change your life. It is from that premise that we are able to explore the thinking behind these ideas and the power with which embracing them will change and direct your focus. This is a shift that will happen over the next few weeks, assuming that you are ready and willing to do this work on yourself.

Being ready is the key. If you aren't ready, no program or book will work. If you are, almost any one will. But being ready needn't be a long, drawn-out process. It is simply a matter of saying you are. As you read this book, think about the things in your own life that will be enhanced as you begin to take charge of your time and your productivity. Imagine how you will feel when things are done in a timely manner, when the stress is gone and you actually have time to live your life.

As an entrepreneur you want to be as efficient and productive as possible so that your business will grow in proportion to your level of increasing knowledge and revenue-producing activities. Managing your time effectively is at the very center of this process. Connie earned a lot more money during her second year as an entrepreneur than she did during her first year, primarily because she had learned so much from others who had come online before her and she was simply able to spend her time engaged in more worthwhile activities. At this time she had her first experience with outsourcing, where she had people who helped her for a few hours each month with the things that no longer required her immediate attention. She also had others actively involved in the parts of her business that she could not do, such as web design, technology, video editing, and graphics. A lesson learned here was that if she could not or would not do it herself, it was time to delegate that task to someone who was capable of doing it better than she ever could, and in much less time. Finally, some of her first year's activities were eliminated altogether as she saw that they did not bring her the ROI (return on investment) that she was hoping for.

Time management, in the world of the entrepreneur, is the art of thinking differently about the twenty-four hours you have each day so that you will accomplish more in both your personal and business life, improve your social and business interactions with friends, family, and colleagues, and have a noticeable increase in your energy level that will be observed by and commented upon by the people around you. One of the things Geoff hears a lot these days is, "Geoff, you seem so calm, lately."

This is an adventure to be sure, but one based on the research findings, life experiences, and "social more" principles that have been discussed in our culture since the turn of the nineteenth century. Yes, what we are discussing here began more than a hundred years ago, and is just as valuable now as it was when your great-grandparents were alive.

As an entrepreneur you are expected to be creative, innovative, and open to experimenting with new ideas that appear in the marketplace. Without proper prioritizing, planning, and implementation you do not stand a chance against the fierce competition coming at you from all directions.

Business is a game, and the most successful people are those who truly love the excitement and adventure of the game. Games are always more fun when we win, so it becomes crucial to our success that we set ourselves up for a win every time by being prepared and ready to play. If you become skilled at managing your time and increasing your productivity, you start out far ahead of the other players. Let's look at a specific example of this.

There are hundreds of ways to learn how to use WordPress as a business tool. WordPress is a content management system used to set up your blog and other websites, manage your membership sites, and for a variety of other uses. People who are just getting started as online entrepreneurs, as well as those who are changing over from previous methods of managing their online content, all need to learn the fundamentals of WordPress, as well as some more advanced techniques. This market extends into the mainstream as more and more people discover the ease and benefits of using this platform to express their ideas and get their messages out to the world.

There are also hundreds of people offering some level of training on how to use WordPress. Their training ranges from a series of short videos offered at no cost on YouTube to a four month intensive training program, with everything you can imagine in between. This high-end course is one that costs more than two thousand dollars for someone to participate in, and it culminates each year with a live event where the participants show off their sites and learn even more ways to market themselves and their business in today's sophisticated landscape.

It is Connie's opinion that everyone who teaches others how to use WordPress should have just one goal: to offer a course that will be considered to be the best one for a variety of reasons, including convenience to the students, completeness of the curriculum, overall cost, level of interaction with the teachers and other students, access to resources, and more. This does not mean that it needs to be the most expensive, taught using the latest technology, or one that covers every aspect of the subject matter. It should just be the best course, in the eyes of the course creator and of the marketplace.

If you are going to do something, be the best you can be in that area. Second best is not worth going for when you're playing the game of business. The winner, the person who is considered the go-to person, is the one who has mastered the use of their time and can be more productive than anyone else who teaches this topic. Everyone else is simply dipping their toe in the water and not living up to their full potential. The 'best' course in this example, like we mentioned above, need not be the one that takes the longest to complete or teaches the most advanced techniques; it only needs to be the one that serves the majority of clients in a way that suits their needs.

In other words, the *market* dictates what is to be offered and at what price, not the product creator. The difference in revenue between the perceived expert in this example and the person who is just making a small effort is in the two million dollars a year range. This has nothing at all to do with the level of intelligence, the years of experience involved, or with the level of connectedness any one of these people might possess; it's all a matter of time management.

Learn how to manage your time and your business will prosper. We have seen this happen repeatedly in our own businesses. We continue to serve our respective clients well because we take the time to find out exactly what they want and then offer it to them in a variety of ways over a period of time. This is leverage in our businesses and makes it much easier for us to grab our fair market share at any time. You will be able to do this as well.

What Are Your Priorities?

"You may as well borrow a person's money as his time."
~Horace Mann

Working from your home can be a dream come true, especially if you come from a background of working for others and having very little time with your family. This was Connie's experience when she made the jump from working as a classroom teacher and a real estate appraiser to working exclusively online. In her past life she had to leave the house each morning before six, and typically did not return home until seven or eight that evening. During the fall and winter months this meant that it was dark outside when she left each day and dark when she got home. Some days she wondered why she even bothered to have a nice home. She was hardly ever there to enjoy it. Have you ever wondered the same thing? How often do you get to enjoy your home, your family, even your solitude?

For both of us, having the opportunity to make our own hours, enjoy our homes each day, and to build a business that we could be involved in for the rest of our lives was a thrill. However, it didn't take long for either of us to realize that the dream was turning into a nightmare as we encountered one interruption after another throughout each day.

For Connie, it seemed like overnight she had become the person her family, friends, and neighbors turned to when they needed something handled during business hours. She was home, after all. She was accepting packages and other deliveries, dropping off and picking up a variety of people from their appointments, and agreeing to have two hour lunches during the middle of the week. What happened? Where did the dream go? For Geoff, the distractions where more of his own making. He has a natural propensity toward shiny things, and working at home gave him lots of shiny things to pursue, like a new book, a new web site, a new personal project, a phone call, an interesting email or seven. The stuff of business wasn't getting done.

The answer to this for both of us was a simple one, as it often is for people who suddenly find themselves with time on their hands and a lack of disciple and structure with their time. Connie had not made it clear to herself and to others in her life that working in her new business was a priority. Once she took a step back from the situation and saw what was going on, she was able to make the necessary changes to become more productive, all by managing her time more efficiently. Geoff's process was the same, except who he had to make it clear to was mostly himself.

When you are working at home, whether you are alone or have a family, it is important to set working hours for your business. One way to think about it is that you are working for someone. Yes, that someone is you, but that someone expects his or her worker to be there on time and get the job done. Make it clear to yourself and your family that you are at work. Even if you have a specific room where you run your business, and do so with the door closed, it's easy for a family member to simply open that door with what they think of as a simple request or question. Make it clear that, when you are in that room with the door closed, you are at work and are not to be bothered by anything less than an earthquake or a fire. Make it clear to yourself, also.

Connie has more energy and ideas early in the morning, so she begins her work-day at seven a.m. each morning, Monday through Friday. She takes a break at nine-thirty, and lunch is from twelve to one. She then continues working until four, with another short break at two in the afternoon. On Fridays she decided to end her work-day at noon, allowing her to go out to lunch or even to a movie on Friday afternoon. She also works on Saturdays from seven in the morning until eleven. This gives her roughly thirty-five hours each week that are devoted exclusively to her business.

Geoff finds he has much more energy and is much more productive in the evenings, so his day is shaped a bit differently, but takes into account that he must have client interaction during the days. It took him a bit to find a balance, but his schedule is now fairly set each day.

Make a chart. Tape it to your door. Email it to your friends and family to let them know when you can be available. If you have a day that you end early, as Connie does, you will find that your lunch openings begin to fill quickly as people who are available during the day snap up this opportunity to spend time with you. Those who work more traditional hours invite Connie to join them on a week night or on a Saturday or Sunday afternoon. You can make similar arrangements.

Your neighbors will soon understand that you are serious about this and find other people to accept their packages and drive them to appointments. Connie spoke to each of her neighbors in person to let them know how important it was to her that her business be successful, and that she would still make herself available to them in cases of emergency.

At the beginning of this section, we asked the question, "What are your priorities?" We have talked a lot about making your business a priority, and that is something we highly recommend, but let's take a step back from that. Let's look at why you are in business.

Many people say they are in business in order to make a difference on the planet, in order to take care of their families, in order to be able to travel, or any of an unlimited amount of things you could mention. The truth is, however, you are in business to make money, and it can be very effective to sit with that for a brief moment.

The money you make will then allow you to make a difference. It will allow you the ability to take care of your family, to travel, to have a garden or collect classic cars. It's the combination of financial freedom and time freedom that makes all things possible. It will allow you to do what you want with your life and to have the life you want, but let's be clear. The business is there to make you money.

When you are clear about that, it makes setting your boundaries much more important. Knowing that also makes it much easier to see what tasks and activities are important, what goals are worthy, and what projects are the ones to tackle.

We'll share a story with you here that you may already be familiar with. It's called "The Big Rocks of Life" and is adapted from a story in *First Things First*, a book by Stephen R. Covey, where he discusses the importance of setting priorities in your life:

A professor of philosophy stood before his class with some items in front of him. When the class began, wordlessly he picked up a large empty mayonnaise jar and proceeded to fill it with rocks about two inches in diameter. He then asked the students if the jar was full.

They agreed that it was full.

So the professor then picked up a box of pebbles and poured them into the jar. He shook the jar lightly and watched as the pebbles rolled into the open areas between the rocks. The professor then asked the students again if the jar was full.

They chuckled and agreed that it was indeed full this time.

The professor picked up a box of sand and poured it into the jar. The sand filled the remaining open areas of the jar. "Now," said the professor, "I want you to recognize that this jar signifies your life. The rocks are the truly important things, such as family, health and relationships.

If all else was lost and only the rocks remained, your life would still be meaningful. The pebbles are the other things that matter in your life, such as work or school. The sand signifies the remaining "small stuff" and material possessions.

We have seen this done in person as a demonstration several times, and once the presenter even had a bottle of water that he poured into the jar over the rocks, pebbles, and sand. This was to signify the things in your life that erode your main priorities and set you back even further.

Think about the priorities you have right now. If you aren't sure what they are, go through your bank statement from last month and see what you spent your money on. Those are your priorities and only you can manage and reorder them to change your life.

This exercise is also powerful to let you know when you have been following priorities that don't necessarily align with what you say you want to do with your life. If you have said that you want to make a difference on the planet, and you discover that you spend most of your time and money shopping for clothing or for movies and games, you now have the opportunity to really look at what you have let your priorities become. Once you know that, you can either adjust those priorities or adjust what you say you are committed to.

Geoff has a friend, a brilliant music teacher. Teaching music to individuals took a set amount of time, and once her schedule was filled, short of raising her prices, she was at her maximum income level. She has also taught others to teach music and has thought for many years that one way to increase her income would be to license her teaching method. That way, more people could learn from her knowledge and she could make more money. Every time Geoff has asked her how setting up that licensing was going, she said she simply didn't have the time to do it. The last time Geoff asked her and she said that, he then asked, besides the actual teaching, what else do you spend your time doing? She started listing things: Scheduling students, cleaning house, reading, going to concerts and plays, etc., etc. It was a long list. She is a very busy woman. As she talked, though, she started to get the idea. If she had the goal to make more money, and wanted to license her techniques in order to do that, it would start to dictate what she spent her time on and her money on.

It turned out a lot of how she spent her time was pleasant but not productive. During the set up of her new business, she could put those things aside in order to concentrate on her new (or newly articulated) priority. Once things were in place, more money would naturally be coming in. Her entire daily routine would be different and finally, she would have much more time to do those pleasant things that, until she sat down and looked at it, had become the priority.

For some of us, when deciding what to do at any given moment, the first thought that comes up, consciously or subconsciously, is, "What will be the most fun?" For some of us, the thought is, "What needs being done right now?" but that's considered without any idea about how it will enhance our lives. We are entrepreneurs. We are in business to make money. We want that money to be able to do any number of things, but when we remember that we are in business to make money, when deciding what the next task should be, the question, "Which one will make me the most money?" might be a very powerful question to ask. It will immediately put into perspective the relative importance of your list of things to do.

You may have heard the saying that 'if you do not have an assistant then you are one'. That statement had a nasty stinging effect the first time Connie heard it, but she realized immediately that it applied to her. She was spending time each week doing a variety of things, including chores, errands, and domestic work that would have been better off being outsourced. She thought about why she was still spending her valuable time doing things that others would do at minimum wage and it dawned on her that she felt unworthy of having paid help to do things related to her home.

She gave herself a few days to think this over and came to the conclusion that she had her priorities out of whack with her financial goals and mission for her business. She stepped back from what she had been doing and allowed others to do the things that were not bringing her the income she wanted and deserved. These actions freed her up to spend her days creating content, products, and services that made the best use of her time.

You will always have things that need to be done in your daily life as well as your business. And, as always, once you have done those things, the others will still be there to do or to delegate.

ACTION STEPS:

Take a look at where you spend most of your money.

Take a look at where you spend most of your time.

If you discover that you aren't focused on what you say are your priorities, think about how you can change that so you can do what will actually move you forward in your life.

Getting Stuff Done Vs. Getting Where You Want To Go

*"Get into the habit of keeping nothing on your mind.
And the way to do that is not by managing time,
managing information, or managing priorities.
It's by managing your actions."*
~David Allen

Achieving optimal productivity and time management is an excellent goal, but first you must decide where it is that you want to go. By this we mean that you must know how you will measure your time and productivity to make sure you're on track. For example, Connie writes short articles each week as part of a goal to create new and relevant content, drive targeted and qualified traffic and visitors to her sites, and to build her list of prospects for the various products and services she offers as a part of her business.

The goal with this for the first couple of years was to write one new article and submit it to the article directories every single day. Now she sees it very differently; the goal is to add five more people to her list every day, and writing articles is just one of the methods she uses to achieve this goal. The articles themselves, while important, aren't the goal. Building the list is.

As entrepreneurs, our days are filled with a variety of tasks and activities that we believe must be completed in order for us to move ahead in our business and increase our bottom line. What we are talking about in this section is the idea that there is always more than one way to look at a situation for it to work in the way that we are imagining that it should. The goal, and we'll be talking more about setting and achieving goals later on in this book, is related to the mission for your business. Connie's mission, for example, as set forth in her Mission Statement, is to help people who are unemployed, underemployed, or dissatisfied with their current work situation to become online entrepreneurs to create a profitable and rewarding business. Geoff's is to help people reawaken their creativity and then use that to enhance their lives and their businesses.

To fulfill your mission it seems to make sense to look at the outcome and desired results of your actions rather than the specific activities you engage in to get there. Allow us to use another example of how this works:

During 2007, Connie decided that it was time for her to earn at least six figures a year in her business. That was what she had been earning while teaching in the classroom and working in real estate part-time, so it made sense that she would need to make at least that much in order to justify this new entrepreneurial effort. She took a look at where she was at that particular moment in time, and then figured out what she could do to increase her income. She had been doing lots of affiliate marketing at the time, so her initial reaction was always to look for what else she could promote in order to earn more money.

This approach had not been working as well as she had hoped, so she knew that expecting different results was not an option. Instead, she came to the conclusion that she needed to create more products of her own, to build relationships with people who could help her in various ways, and to attend more live events in her industry if she wanted to significantly increase her bottom line.

Within six months she had created six new products, reached out to twenty people through social media, and signed up to attend two live events to connect with influential people in her industry. In the three months that followed she had increased her income more than fifty percent, taking her well over the six figures a year threshold.

We want to emphasize that this did not happen by slogging away at a computer more hours each day. In fact, during this period she began working fewer hours each week so that she could have more time for creative thinking and planning, something we refer to as daydreaming. As a teacher Connie was supposed to break children from the habit of daydreaming; as an entrepreneur it was the very thing that was needed as a daily productivity booster.

We describe daydreaming as the act of sitting with yourself. This is best done alone, with no outside stimuli or interruptions of any kind. You allow your mind to wander to a faraway place where you are in charge and do things exactly as you believe they should be done. There is no one there with a better idea and all things you imagine during this time are perfect for you and what you want to do. It's a very selfish time. Deliciously selfish, in fact, to the point of giving you the opportunity to become your best self, and to be able to give back to others in a way that has been impossible in the past. As you develop and strengthen your daydreaming muscle you will understand which actions to take and how to manage those actions in a ways that further your ability to achieve empowered goals in your life.

Managing our actions is the key to real productivity. David Allen, in his book *Getting Things Done: The Art of Stress-Free Productivity*, states that people often believe that lack of time is their problem, when actually it is a lack of clarity of what the project really is and what the required next steps need to be.

Getting things done each day has little value, unless you are taking the bigger picture into consideration and only engaging in activities that can work to help you achieve your goals. Think of this as 'beginning with the end in mind'. This refers to the belief that we must know our final destination if we are to get there from where we are today. Your final destination may be to relocate to a new city, or to build your dream home in the city where you currently live, or to donate to a charity that has personal meaning and significance in your life. By thinking of this destination you can step back and decide what steps will be necessary to take you from where you currently are to where you'd like to be.

It is very easy to get caught up in busy work, because, well, that stuff just needs to get done. Stop and take a step back for a moment. Remember what the actual goal is. Now look at the tasks ahead with that in mind and you will find yourself doing things in a very different way.

ACTION STEPS:

Spend some time thinking about the life you would love to create for yourself. How would you spend each day?

Look at how you spend your day now. What tasks are being done that will help you get to your goal? Think about how you can focus more on those.

Which ones are being done simply to get them done? Think about whether they need to be done, and if they do, how you could get them done either more quickly or by someone else so you can focus on the things that will move you toward your goals.

Section II: What Is Time Management?

"We are what we repeatedly do. Excellence, then, is not an act, but a habit."
~Aristotle

We've been talking about time management for many pages, now, but what exactly *is* time management? We all have the same twenty-four hours each day, yet some of us find that we are able to do everything we want and need to do while others constantly feel pressed for time. There is no secret to this, but one thing is clear: planning out your time in advance and having structure and a routine in your daily life will definitely allow you more freedom to be creative and to accomplish more.

This makes sense if you stop to think about it. Anything that is creative in nature, such as writing, running a business, or creating information products (these are examples from our world as online marketers) requires discipline, persistence, and consistency in order to be successful.

It may seem counterintuitive that creativity requires structure and discipline. We often think of creativity as that chaotic, un-harnessable energy that strikes at its own whim and desire. The actual truth, however, is that creativity is a habit and to get that habit takes structure and discipline. When you are in the habit of creating, when you create whether you feel like it or not, you are actually opening yourself up to brilliance. If you sit around waiting for inspiration to hit, you'll probably be asleep if and when it does.

Let's use the writing of this book as an example. Connie was recommending a program on writing books for Kindle to her subscribers. The program was not too expensive – less than three hundred dollars – and the commitment was more about taking the time to write the book than on spending lots of money to learn how to do it. On a Saturday morning, September 1, 2012, she made the decision to write this book, contacted Geoff to see if he wanted to come aboard the project as a co-author, and then it was off the ground. Luckily, Geoff excitedly agreed to what she was proposing, or the goal most likely would have needed to be modified accordingly. (That's another great point, by the way. Circumstances change. When they do, the plan must be adjusted. With the end goal in mind, what to adjust and how to adjust it will become obvious.)

Several hours later we had both done research on the topic of time management and productivity, looked through a dozen or so books on this by reputable authors, and had outlined the chapters we would include. We sent each other our notes and combined them. On Sunday we had each begun writing, and by Monday the book was half completed. We emailed each other the sections we had written, made adjustments, each added our own thoughts, discussed it briefly on the phone, and went back to work.

Our original goal was to write this book from start to finish with an edited manuscript, based on neither of us using any content we had previously written on anything related to the subject matter, and to have it published and available for sale on Kindle within seven days. As you can see, if you take a look at the publication date, we easily achieved our goal of publishing this book on September 8, 2012.

It's important to note that both of us were in the middle of several other projects related to our respective businesses, as well as activities planned with friends and family as it was a holiday weekend (Labor Day in the United States). We have both found it possible to add a new project to our plates, while not giving up other work or pleasure to get it finished in a timely manner.

We also naturally divided the project into parts, where each of us used our area of strength to fulfill the needs of what we were working to accomplish. Geoff is talented when it comes to graphics and design, so he took on the task of creating a cover that would work well on the Kindle and in the Amazon marketplace. He also has the gift of editing and formatting and assumed this role as well. Connie loves keywords, so she went about doing the research on which keyword phrases should be included in the title of the book to have it rank higher in the search engines.

We believe this ability to complete a major project in such a short period of time is directly proportionate to how successful we have been over the past few years with goal setting and achieving, increased productivity, and management of our time. There is absolutely no reason at all that you can't do the same thing in every area of your own life and business.

By respecting and valuing your time, you place an emphasis on it in every area of your life. The people around you will quickly pick up on this and will modify their behavior accordingly. In Connie's previous life people wanted to 'hang out' and spend time with meaningless activities, such as long phone calls about nothing in particular, endless hours of watching television, and many hours walking through the local shopping malls. She still finds it interesting that we speak about 'spending' time as we do in regards to 'spending' money. If you value your money you most certainly must value your time. These days her phone calls are short and to the point, the television is rarely on and anything watched has been recorded from a previous time, and much of the shopping is done online.

Much of this has to do with something called 'time shifting', where you choose to be involved with something of interest to you based on your personal time schedule, not on anyone else's schedule.

Time management is about structure, discipline, and creativity. Author Stephen Denning, in *The Leader's Guide to Storytelling: Mastering the Art and Discipline of Business Narrative*, states that structure is necessary because structure and creativity have the same parentage. As we said above, it is structure that enables creativity. In the great human creations, in the twelve notes of the musical scale, in the twenty-six letters of the alphabet, these fantastic structural inventions have unlocked the enormous creativity of literature and music. Without structure, there is nothing for creativity to get leverage upon.

For an entrepreneur, time management is an important part of that structure.

Productivity and Goals

Goal setting and achieving is one of the most controversial topics of all in the time management and productivity conversation. We have done extensive reading and research into this area, and have incorporated many different systems into both of our daily lives to see what might work best for different people under a variety of circumstances. We have both come to the conclusion that simply setting goals that are not supported or emphasized on a daily basis is a futile attempt to bring order out of chaos and does little to move us forward. In fact, it will frustrate us and will actually be counterproductive. These become little more than New Year's resolutions, cast aside and forgotten within days of the New Year. Goals set without looking at them in terms of what we really want to achieve in our lives and in our businesses very quickly become pointless exercises and we will abandon them.

On the other hand, writing down specific goals that relate to what we wish to achieve as part of our life's mission and vision are worthwhile and hold the promise of a more rewarding and satisfying life experience.

Getting back to the example of how this book came to be written and published in only seven days, we will share with you that Connie always writes down her goals in a tangible format. On her small yellow legal pad she wrote:

"I will write and publish a book on time management and productivity this week. I will ask Geoff to be my co-author to bring his expertise and experience into the writing and the project as a whole. The book will be eighty pages in length, with twenty thousand words, and will be divided into ten chapters."

Throughout the week she read, reread, changed, modified, and expanded upon this original goal. The eighty pages turned into a hundred and the twenty thousand words became more negotiable by mid-week. It was now a matter of producing a final product they would both be proud to have their names on and to include as part of their online business funnels.

But look clearly at even that original goal. In the previous section, we talked about what our priorities were. The priority that the goal of this book falls under is furthering our business. It will also have the wonderful effect of helping many people begin to transform the way they look at their own time management, but the initial goal was simply to further our businesses.

Once Connie made the decision to use this book to further that goal, then enrolled Geoff in the process, getting it done became a simple matter of seeing the end product and working backwards, something referred to as 'reverse engineering'. This means that they had to start with the end in mind and then see the steps in a backward movement (in reverse order) to see which actions would logically come before each one they had already completed. In order to have a book uploaded to Kindle by the end of the week, certain things had to happen each day. Once we knew what those things were, it was a simple matter to sit down and do them. The goal created the productivity. Nothing we were engaged in during the process of writing this book was busy work. Every task was, as they say in the business training videos, on point. It is immediately obvious if a task presents itself that won't result in the book being done, and it gets pushed aside.

Even the tasks that are for other goals become part of the process. For instance, Geoff had made a commitment to have one of his client's web sites done this weekend. That was a commitment that he would never renege on. He knew he had to structure the weekend in such a way that both things got accomplished. The goals were compatible, they both involved furthering his business, and they both got accomplished. He set about working on the web site with the goal of the book also in mind, and it helped him focus on the specific tasks need to accomplish it and made very clear any task that would get in the way.

Connie had also promised her favorite Aunt and Uncle, a couple in their eighties, that they could come for a visit on Sunday and Monday and that she would prepare some of their favorite dishes while they were at her house. She made some notes about what they wanted to eat, what else they would want to do while they were there, and what their typical daily schedule entailed. Because they like to sleep late and Connie gets up very early each day, it was easy for her to schedule the time to write and still spend lots of time with them. They also wanted to visit with another couple they've known for many years during their stay, so she was able to arrange that and give herself two additional hours to write. Everything came together nicely, and her aunt and uncle enjoyed hearing about the new book she was working on. She even read them several passages from the book and asked them what they thought about it. Connie learned long ago that involving others in what you are working on makes them much more likely to be supportive of the time and effort involved in completing a project.

Goals in and of themselves are not a bad thing. In fact, making a goal for yourself is an excellent starting point for taking action on a direction or project that will move you forward in your life. But do not delude yourself into thinking that if you set a goal, either by saying it out loud to another person or writing it down, that it has much of a chance of being achieved. Instead, think of the written goal as the first piece of the blueprint that you will develop over time to get yourself on track to succeed in this area.

Connie writes down her goals at the first of each month in six different areas. She has done this since July of 2005 and credits this system with changing her thinking and turning her life around. These six areas are:

- Main goal for the month – This is different each month and can encompass anything that needs to be done in your life, such as cleaning out the garage, creating a new product, buying a piece of property, taking an extended vacation, etc.

- Acknowledgement – This is where you write down the names of several people who have helped you during the previous month and then contact them to acknowledge them personally for what they have done for you.

- Increase in Wealth – This is what you will be doing during the current month to increase your overall wealth by the beginning of the next month.

- New – This is something new you will do to improve yourself, such as running in a 5K race, wearing dress shoes instead of sneakers to business events from now on, or getting a manicure once a month.

- Learn – This is something brand new you decide to pursue, such as country line dancing, learning to speak a new language, or going through a ropes course.

- You – This is something you do just for yourself, like going to the theatre or a concert, spending the weekend at the beach, or spending an afternoon sitting in your favorite chair while sipping a frothy drink and listening to some music.

Writing these down simply anchors them in time; the real work comes once she gets into action and starts implementing each step in the process of achieving the goal.

ACTION STEPS:

With your mission statement in mind (what you want to accomplish in your life – more on that in the next section), write out goals within these six areas for the next month for yourself.

Take that list and start planning what tasks need to be done to accomplish them.

Knowing Where You Want To Go

"What lies behind us and what lies before us are tiny matters compared to what lies within us."
~Oliver Wendell Holmes

In day to day life we all encounter people who are simply allowing life to lead them along, like sheep keeping up with the flock. When you ask them questions such as where they will be going on vacation or which college their son or daughter might be applying to, they just look at you with blank stares.

We've touched on this already, but when you know where you want to go, it is much easier to get there. That sounds like a joke, but it's true. If you don't know where you want to go, you will be stuck doing busy work and lots will be done, but nothing will be accomplished. This reminds us of a quote by Lewis Carroll in Alice in Wonderland where White Rabbit says, "The hurrier I go the behinder I get."

Let's look at how you can know where you want to go. We talked about our mission statements. Figuring yours out can be a very powerful thing to do.

Start by asking yourself what you would like your life to look like on a daily basis. What would you be doing? Who would be there with you? How would you earn money? What causes or groups would you be of service to? Connie knew that she wanted to be able to work from home, to still feel like a teacher, and to have the time and money to volunteer her time and to donate to charities and non-profit service organizations. With that as her guiding thought she pursued the life of an online entrepreneur and now works with people on six continents to help them to start their own home based businesses.

Geoff has always loved watching people discover their own potential and start striving to reach it. All of his life, he has helped people do this and when he sees someone doing it, whether he had anything to do with it or not, it moves him, sometimes to tears. As a writer, even when he writes fiction, a big part of the thrust of what he writes is about how people can discover who the really are (or even invent who they really could be) and then set about doing that. When he sat down to say what his mission statement might be, this passion was forefront in his mind. He realized that this is something people want and are willing to pay for. It already encompasses making a difference on the planet and in people's lives. When he looks for places to spend his charity time, helping people reach their potential is never far from his thoughts. When he puts out a new book, guiding people, directly or subtly, to discover they can be more and reach further is always a main part of the thrust.

Remember in the introduction, we mentioned that there were times when Geoff was very successful in managing his time? In almost all of those occasions, it was when he was involved in something that would help people realize their potential or stretch who they thought they could be. When directing a theatre piece, it was specifically the actors but also the potential audience. When working for the law firm, it was the secretaries, yes, but also the firm itself and its clients. Being able to help the firm fulfill its purpose really motivated him.

Connie can remember her days as a classroom teacher when everything was so unclear. The administrators at the school typically mapped out a plan for your future and expected you to fall into place and accept your destiny. When it was suggested that she leave the classroom and take an administrative position in downtown Los Angeles she shuddered at the thought. Connie could not understand why anyone would want to work for a school district and not work with children every day. It became clear that her mission in regards to working in the education field was not in alignment with what her superiors had in mind for her future. It was seen as a weakness in character to stay in the public school system and not aspire to leave the classroom for a higher position. It wasn't until she began to manage her time and think about her productivity that her life truly began to change and she had the confidence to make decisions that were the right ones for her.

Geoff's commitment to helping people see who they are, despite some early floundering trying to figure it out, now dictates pretty much everything he does in his business and his personal life.

Even thinking about writing down your mission statement might sound daunting, but it is so important. It shouldn't take you very long, and, as with everything, it will probably change and evolve some as the years go by, but having that guiding document will be invaluable in helping you know, on an almost moment-to-moment basis, which actions to pursue and which actions to leave behind. This is almost the very definition of time management.

As an entrepreneur, you probably already have a sense of what your mission might be, but getting it clear is vital. The first thing to think about when building your mission statement is to look at the things you do and have done very well. Many times we have great difficulty in seeing ourselves as others see us when it comes to figuring this out. When Connie was first online she could not determine what she had to offer others that would make her unique and able to stand out from the crowd. When she asked her family and close friends what they thought she was good at, they could not believe she did not see her strengths. They reminded her that she was the person they came to when they needed to write something, whether it was for work or for personal reasons. They recounted stories of how she had been the one to help them write a eulogy when someone close to them had passed, or how she had helped them to edit and rewrite their essay for the class they took years ago to finish their college degree. Connie listened intently as they took turns sharing, and then encouraged them to go on.

One by one the people she had gathered that evening told her what she was good at and what they thought of when they thought about her. Connie was the person they trusted to advise them on buying a new computer. She was the one who walked them step by step through the process of learning a new piece of computer software. She was there for them when they needed to write something and could not decide where to begin. That was when she made the decision to start her online career as someone who made technology simple and who helped people write articles, blog posts, and eBooks. She was on a mission to help people in these areas!

A lot of people talk about the need to follow your passion, but that's not quite what we're talking about here. How you structure your mission statement should incorporate what you are passionate about, but it should also have a practical side. Being passionate about butterflies is fine, but we are talking about building a business that will make us the money to do what we want, so if butterflies won't do that for you, find something that will. And once you have your business in place and focused, you can study butterflies all you want.

While both of our missions involve helping other people, yours doesn't necessarily need to be that. Many people say they want to make a million dollars, but have no idea what that really means, have no passion for it besides that it sounds really good, and wouldn't really know what to do with it if they actually got the money. For most of us, that is a very empty motivator and won't move us forward at all. However, if your mission truly is to be able to retire to a villa on an island in the Pacific, that's fine, just know that there will be a lot of work between now and then to create the funds to be able to do that. It takes a lot of work to create a life of leisure.

And there really are some people who are very, very motivated simply by the desire to have money. There is nothing wrong with this. Just be honest with yourself. We suspect this isn't the case for most people and if you won't really be motivated by that seemingly logical notion, set it aside as a pretty thought and find out what really motivates you, what you really want to accomplish in your life.

If your mission is something completely charitable, eradicating malaria in Africa, for example, or poverty in America, you may think pursuing a business that has the purpose of making money is at odds with that. However, upon closer examination, look at the people who are actually doing things like this. Almost without exception, they are people who made a lot of money, which enabled them to do these very worthy things. If that really is your mission (and again, be honest, it may sound romantic but may not be true for you), design your business, and therefore the tasks you must accomplish, with that in mind, but know that the business is there to make the money so that it becomes possible. For certain people, a mission like that can really motivate them.

And for some, the mission is simply and powerfully the ability to take care of and spend time with their family. Again, really look to see if this is true for you, though. For many who say this is their motivation, they are simply echoing what others around them have said is a worthy goal. Yes, it is a worthy goal, but it may not be your mission. Don't let your family or your parents or your community dictate what your mission is. It is your mission, not theirs.

Your mission statement shouldn't be too complex. Many of us complicate things to the point that they become useless. As you structure your mission statement, it will become clear that it is what you are already committed to. It will ring with a resonant sound. If it doesn't quite ring, adjust it until it does. Writing a mission statement is often more about discovering what is already there rather than creating something new. But writing it down makes it specific so you can then use it to support everything you do.

Don't spend all of your time on this. It is important, but as a support, not as the goal itself. It is the destination, it is not the map, nor is it the road you will be traveling. Once you have it, though, that road becomes much clearer. Managing your time becomes much more second nature.

ACTION STEPS:

Think about what you have always thought you should be doing with your life.

Write down why you decided to be (or want to be) an entrepreneur.

From the above, draft a simple mission statement. It doesn't have to be the final draft, and probably won't be for a while, and it doesn't have to be a masterpiece of writing, but get it written down.

Now begin to look at what you are doing in your life and your business that supports that mission and what you are doing that doesn't.

Do more of what does and start getting rid of what doesn't.

Section III:
How Does Time Management Work In A Step By Step Process?

"You'll never 'find' time for anything. If you want time, you must make it."
~Charles Bruxton

Time management is defined as the act or process of planning and exercising conscious control over the amount of time spent on specific activities, especially to increase effectiveness, efficiency or productivity, and at times assisted by various skills, methods, tools, and techniques.

We've talked about goals, we've talked about your mission. It should be becoming clear that, the more you know where you are going, the easier it is to find the path to get there. Time management, then, is the process you use to do that.

Once you know where you're going, what you want to accomplish, whether it is the ultimate goal of your life or what you want to accomplish in the next several years, work backwards from there.

Sometimes a creative and innovative method of managing the step by step processes in a specific field in order to save time and to become more productive are born out of a necessity to help someone else. This is exactly what happened with the Khan Academy. In case you have not heard about this, we will share the story with you here.

In 2004 a New Orleans seventh grader named Nadia found herself struggling in her math class. She asked her older cousin, hedge fund analyst Sal Khan, if he could help her. Sal lived in Boston, so he began using something called Doodle Notepad to work with her interactively each evening for thirty minutes or so during the week. Soon Nadia's grades and confidence had risen, and her brothers and other cousins wanted Sal to help them with their math lessons as well. We should tell you that Sal has degrees in mathematics, electrical engineering, and computer science, so he was more than qualified to help them with their junior high level math homework.

However, Sal was busy with work and with his own young family, so he decided to start making videos to answer their questions and then post them to YouTube so the other family members could benefit as well. This is an important part of the story, because what he was doing was managing his time more efficiently by doing something once and sharing it with a small group of people.

As he continued to tutor Nadia and the others in this way, people searching for answers to their math homework began to find the videos on YouTube. Within a couple of years Sal became known for his teaching methods and for making difficult mathematics much easier to understand. During this time he had refined his techniques to the point that he could explain highly advanced and complicated equations in a way that took much less time than anyone had ever been able to do in the past.

His original mission was to provide help to just one person, Nadia, but now has become to provide "tens of thousands of videos in pretty much every subject" to people all over the world. His greater vision is to create "the world's first free, world-class virtual school where anyone can learn anything".

Non-profit organizations have distributed offline versions of his videos to rural areas of Africa, Latin America, and Asia, and in 2010 Bill Gates, Microsoft founder and philanthropist, shared that he was using Sal's videos, now distributed through his non-profit company called the Khan Academy, to help his own children with their mathematics homework during the school year and with their overall education while not at school.

The Bill and Melinda Gates Foundation and Google have recognized him for his work and have now given him significant backing. In 2012 Sal Khan was featured on the

CBS television show '60 Minutes' and he was listed among the *Time 100 Most Influential People for 2012*.

When you think back to how this came about, it was based on his ability to manage his time by teaching several people at a time instead of just one-on-one training, to find faster, more efficient ways to learn complex subject matter, and to distribute this information and training to the uneducated masses as a means of increasing efficiency and productivity throughout the world. If one man can educate a billion people all at once, just imagine how you can increase your productivity and manage your time if you make an effort to increase your own time management skills.

Short-Term Vs. Long-Term Planning

Once you know where you are going, the planning to get there becomes much easier. You have the destination in mind when you set your plans down. However, the further in the future those plans are, the more general they will have to be because things change over time.

There are two pitfalls that many people will fall into. One is to focus so much on the long-term that nothing ever gets done today. Yes, having a long-term goal is vital, but it is difficult for the human mind to really grasp the specifics of something that far out in time. Again, the mission or goal is there to guide you, to guide and shape the decisions you make, the plans you set out to accomplish. It is what you measure your plans against.

The other side is extreme short-term thinking. Either trying to plan things out in an impossibly complex, almost moment-to-moment way, or living "paycheck-to-paycheck." We'll talk about that in a moment, but the micro, moment-to-moment planning will often get you in trouble. When stated like that, it becomes obvious why this might not work, but if you are someone who attempts this, you might do well to examine if it has ever been very effective. This kind of planning can be more chaos-inducing than not having a plan at all. You are spending so much time planning that the actual doing won't get done. Also, this kind of planning can become rigid and any change in circumstance will completely frustrate you because it has such an extreme effect on so much that you have labored to set down. You will resist adjusting to the new circumstance, often going as far as to completely ignoring the new circumstance, and everything from that moment forward will be a fight.

Also, with this sort of micro planning, the vital long-term thinking is easily pushed out because the individual tasks become more important than the goal, more important than your mission.

There is, of course, a wonderful compromise. Once you have your end goal in mind, once you have your mission clear, take a chunk of time that is actually manageable and make plans for that.

Connie likes to create actionable goals at the first of every month. She then proceeds to plan out her business life every quarter, with regular updates, changes, and adjustments throughout each three month period. This works particularly well for her online business, where she is constantly scheduling teleseminars and webinars with others, as well as booking her own trainings and creating new products and courses.

However, this plan falls within a much longer view of her life. She knows what her mission is, to help people become online entrepreneurs and to create their own profitable and rewarding businesses. She has a long-term idea of what that will look like. That, of course, is much more flexible than the quarterly plan, but it informs her quarterly plans and helps her build her quarterly plans.

Many people tend to have very short-term thinking. We mentioned living paycheck-to-paycheck. Many of us do this most of our lives and when we do, we are easily distracted by outside forces, which include other people, the media, and events outside of our control. The result is an almost constant state of crisis and wasted time, which leads to frustration, emptiness, and failure to achieve success in life.

Connie found herself caught up in this lifestyle for many years, especially while she was working as a classroom teacher and was paid once a month. She would often find herself short of money for three or four days before it was time for payday to come around once again. It wasn't until she read something from Stephen R. Covey that she began to see the light. Covey had created something called the Time Management Matrix. He went into great detail with this in his book *The 7 Habits of Highly Effective People*, but we wanted to touch upon this concept here to get you started along this line of thinking.

Covey created this matrix as a four quadrant box, where the boxes are labeled:

- Important-Urgent – this would include crises situations and true emergencies

- Important-Not Urgent – this would include prevention, planning, personal growth, relationship building
- Not Important-Urgent – this would include most emails and phone calls
- Not Important-Not Urgent – this would include busy work and other time wasters

The first quadrant is about issues that arise in your life that absolutely must be dealt with immediately.

The second quadrant is one of personal productivity and power, where you can spot opportunities and build long term success.

The third quadrant is where things grab your attention but have little meaning in your life, like when you receive an email about something you need to purchase right now. Geoff spent a lot of time in this box.

The fourth quadrant is about waste; time and resource wasters that you must avoid.

From this simplistic overview we hope you can see that the majority of your time must be spent in the second quadrant, where situations and circumstances are important but not urgent, in order to create a life that will take you to the next level in your personal evolution. We would encourage you to learn more from Stephen R. Covey's excellent materials after you complete this book.

It takes approximately twenty-one days to make or break a habit. Think of activities in your life that waste your time and others that build success for your future. As you begin to plan your days and weeks ahead, choose one habit to break and one to solidify in your life. Connie used to watch television and movies every evening for about two hours. Because she lives alone this became a way to pass the time in the late evenings. When she broke that habit she gained almost two full workdays each week. She replaced that time wasting activity with one of seeing either one movie or one play each week with someone she wanted to get to know better in her city. The result has been a combination of meeting new, interesting people, more networking opportunities, increased business, and a feeling of higher self-worth in her community. Turning off her television and getting out of the house made a huge difference in her life.

Geoff also turned off his television. More accurately, he turned off his DirecTV satellite service. This was done many years ago. The only time he misses it, now, are when there are special presentations like the Oscars or the Olympics that don't stream on the Internet. In terms of short-term and long-term thinking, we are often swayed by the pleasures of the moment. Especially in modern Western society, we are taught that the immediate pleasure is paramount. In our society, we have worked hard to be able to have those pleasures. This is something we don't even often questions. At eight o'clock on Thursday, my favorite television show is on. I must watch it, because it makes me feel good.

This kind of thinking often invades everything we do and can really wreak havoc on our time management. Or, more accurately, on our ability to create the life we say we want, which is what is behind our desire to manage our time. This is very short-term thinking. Neither of us is suggesting that anyone forgo pleasure. What would life be without the things we enjoy? However, when you start with the long-term goal, mission or vision in mind, some of those immediate pleasures begin to lose their appeal.

Begin with the long-term, then bring that closer in. If we say our mission is to help people build profitable home businesses or build our villa on that island or spend more quality time with our family (long-term thinking), then how will watching this television show right now, or reading this book right now (short-term thinking), align with that?

Yes, we both have television shows we love. Mad Men is brilliantly written. Merlin is a guilty pleasure. However, rather than plan our day or week around these tasks, consider using them as rewards for getting closer to our long-term desires. Once you have finished the tasks for the day or week, pop in a DVD of your favorite show, or play the DVR recording of it. (This is the definition of Time Shifting, by the way, which we talked about in Section II. Do things on your schedule, not the television networks'. And do them for your purposes, not anyone else's.)

We're not picking on television, just using it as an example. We often get so caught up in the pleasure of the moment that we lose site of the gift of our lives. We have the habit of "vegging" at the end of the day or on the weekend (which is not the same as daydreaming, by the way, when we veg, we turn our minds off, when we daydream, we turn them on), when we could be using this same time as part of what will give us the life we say we want.

We are also not talking about becoming work-a-holics! This is not managing your time, and if you do it, it will burn you out very quickly. However, as we have said, once we have made clear what our mission is, the decisions on how to spend our time become very easy and some things just naturally drop away, or lose some of their importance, and it becomes very clear what activity we should engage in next and what one after that. It becomes natural and organic, rather than a struggle.

Time Chunking - Breaking Down The End Goal Into Tasks

"I love deadlines. I love the whooshing noise they make as they go by."
~Douglas Adams

You may have heard the joke about how you go about feeding an elephant. The answer, of course, is 'one bite at a time'. But this concept falls well within our discussion here. Just how do you accomplish a large goal or task, when it seems so overwhelming right now? The answer is to do something called 'chunking it down' where you look at the end goal and then break it down into bite size 'chunks' that can be accomplished in a far shorter period of time and with greater ease. Using this idea, you never look at the overall goal except at the very beginning and at the end. In between, you simply go through each step of what needs to be done in order to move on to the next step of the process.

Connie is a linear thinker and action taker, so it works best for her to make a list, reorder that list, and then to keep moving through the list until she is finished.

Geoff is much more holographic, keeping the whole picture in his head while he moves forward, seeing how each move affects that picture. Even he uses lists, however, when he plans his strategy to attack something, but his lists usually start out as random thoughts sort of thrown at a piece of paper, then reorganized and shaped until they start to form a story in his head that he can follow.

For example, when it came to writing this book over a seven day period Connie made a list of the topics she wanted to cover and some notes about each topic. She then organized this list into one that seemed to make sense to her. The next logical step was to email it to Geoff to see what he thought about the list she had started. She trusts him to look at things in a way that is very different from her perspective. As soon as he had tweaked it and made some additional notes he sent it back to her and she started writing.

When Geoff got Connie's list, he immediately saw what the end product could look like and started jotting down ideas about it. He took notes about the cover, did some research about the topic, etc., added his thoughts to Connie's list and sent it back to her. This may seem like a contradiction, that Geoff isn't chunking down at all, but in truth, that is exactly what he's doing. Once he has the picture, the end goal, in mind, he starts tearing that down into bit parts and looking at what needs to be done to accomplish each of those bits.

The difference between Connie's approach and Geoff's is that Connie thinks in terms of the work she wants to be involved in whereas Geoff is more of a 'big picture' person. And Connie is smart enough to know that when she pitches an idea to Geoff and he gets very excited that she has hit upon something that will have great promise. When you find someone that you can relate to in this way a type of magic happens that you will want to create over and over, if at all possible.

There are several techniques that you can use to help you chunk things down.

One is called the Pomodoro Technique® that you might find useful. It was created by a man named Francesco Cirillo in 1992 as a way for him to improve his study habits while in college. The word 'pomodoro' is Italian for tomato (it was named for the tomato shaped kitchen timer first used by Cirillo while he was still a student). The idea with this method is to set the timer for twenty-five minutes, work on your task until the timer goes off, and to then enjoy a five minute rest break until starting another Pomodoro. If you go for four Pomodoros (four twenty-five minute task periods) then you are entitled to a longer break of fifteen or twenty minutes. Personally, both Connie and Geoff have found a Pomodoro to be too short a time for what we typically like to accomplish in one sitting before taking a break, but this may work well for you. And notice that both of us do take breaks. As Geoff often says, step away from the computer. If you work for too long a time without a break, you become fuzzy and much less productive. You can discover where that point is for you, but make sure you include regular breaks throughout your working day.

Timeboxing is another technique used in the time management arena to allot specific amounts of time to specific activities. Rather than have the deadline be moveable, the look of the end product is. This technique can really help if you have a tendency, like Geoff often does, of being a bit of a perfectionist. The idea is to set a specific amount of time for a specific task. This set amount of time should be a firm commitment. To use a fourteen dollar word, inviolable. (Side note from Connie: the official definition of inviolable is 'never to be broken, infringed, or dishonored'.) The only thing, then, that can change is the final "quality" of the task. This doesn't mean it should be shoddy. It just may not be perfect. It will be done and it will be usable.

You may be wondering where multitasking fits in with the scheme of things when it comes to time management and productivity. The answer is that it does not. There is actually no such thing as multitasking because the brain cannot process two sets of data simultaneously. When you attempt to do two things at once you are simply going back and forth between the two activities. Many of us have become quite skilled at this back and forth, but if it feels like you are running in circles as you go about your daily business, it's because you are not giving your focused attention to one thing at a time.

This all comes down to three things:

1. Prioritizing – deciding what you want to accomplish in the next week, month, quarter, or year

2. Planning – chunking it down into doable activities of various lengths

3. Performing – actually doing it!

For example, as Connie sits writing her part of this book it is Saturday afternoon on a holiday weekend (Labor Day in the United States). She realized at ten minutes until three that she wanted to prepare some food and then come back upstairs to do some more writing. She made a short list of what she wanted to do and it looked like this:

- Check to see if I have eggs to do some baking and cucumbers and tomatoes to make a salad
- Make corn bread from a mix
- Make brownies from a mix
- Prepare spaghetti
- Boil corn on the cob
- Prepare lunch for family – leftover beef from roast, baked beans, corn
- Do all of this within one hour and return to my writing

She went downstairs and immediately got the others involved. Preparing food and spending time with people she love is joyous to her, so she wanted this to be fun. She knew that the corn bread and brownies would take the longest to bake – about forty minutes – so that's what she started with. she turned the oven to 375° Fahrenheit, mixed up the corn bread batter and the brownie mix, and put both in to cook.

In the meantime she had added water to two large pots on the stove so they would begin to boil. One was for the spaghetti, which would take just six minutes to cook, and the other was for the corn on the cob, which needed to have at a rapid boil so that the corn could add the eight minutes.

As all of this was taking place she cooked the ground sirloin in a frying pan on the stove and opened up the two jars of sauce for the spaghetti.

She checked on the corn bread and brownies in the oven, drained the spaghetti, stirred the pot with the corn on the cob, opened the can of baked beans and put them in the microwave, and stirred the ground sirloin to see how much longer this might take. Then she took the salad and two bottles of salad dressing out of the refrigerator, chopped up two tomatoes and a cucumber to add to it, and placed the bowl on the table.

At three-thirty she heated up the leftover roast, took the beans out of the microwave, and took out the two earns of corn. She then added the other two ears to the boiling water, made a mental note of when eight more minutes would be up, placed the food on the table, and called everyone to sit down and eat.

As the family finished eating, she turned off the pan of boiling water with the other corn in it, removed the corn bread from the oven, and added the ground sirloin and sauce to the spaghetti.

Right at four o'clock she told everyone she was going back to work, and as she walked away she could see them letting the dogs back in, putting the top on the spaghetti, starting to clear the table and do the dishes, and remove the brownies from the oven. Her work was done, and she had just spent a full hour with the people she loves, doing things together as a family.

She loves to cook, but she doesn't like to shop, clean up, or put things away. Her family has done this for so long that she can now use this idea of timeboxing, where she allows one hour each day during the week and two separate one hour block of time on the weekends for preparing meals and eating food they all enjoy. Of course she deviates from this on a regular basis because she is traveling and involved with other activities in the community, but for the most part this is what works well at her house. She also cook healthier foods much of the time, but if she's writing a book in just seven days something has to give!

It all flows smoothly as long as she delegates the parts that she does not like to do and have the support and cooperation of others. Once you share your desires and expectations with the people around you it's amazing how things fall into place nicely so that everyone benefits.

ACTION STEPS:

Write down a goal you have wanted to accomplish for some time, such as writing a book, creating a new product, starting a membership site, planning a trip with your family, enrolling in a course of study, or anything else you can think of in your personal or business life.

Now, make a list of the steps you must take in order to get there from where you are right now.

Start a To-Do list that includes these steps

Start doing your To-Do list

Section IV:
What If You Utilize These Strategies In Your Life And Business?

"Time you enjoyed wasting is not wasted time."
~T.S. Elliot

Utilizing these strategies in your life and your business will bring you an inner peace that is unlike anything you may have experienced. Imagine being able to plan a trip or create something new in your business, knowing that you will be able to accomplish your goal and see it through to completion without becoming stressed, overwhelmed, or afraid that something will go wrong along the way.

Let's take a closer look at this concept. We have talked a lot about the end goal, the overriding mission for your business. When you know what that is, or at the very least, have a fairly good idea what that is, you can create sub-goals that align with that. Remember, the purpose for any business it to make money. The purpose of that money can be any number of things.

Once you have your ultimate mission, and you have sub-goals that support and lead you toward that mission, look at your sub-goals. What must be accomplished becomes obvious. Prioritizing them becomes really easy. Which ones will make me the most money? Which ones will move me closest toward my overall goal. Those are the tasks to focus on. Do those.

We'd like to share something about the Pareto Principle with you now. This is also known as the 80-20 Rule, and states that 80% of effects come from 20% of causes. This principle, as it relates to our discussion of time management and productivity, has its basis in the tenet that you will spend about twenty percent of your time producing eighty percent of your profits. If this is indeed true, then wouldn't it make sense for all of us to focus on increasing our efficiency with time and efforts directed at producing the financial results we want for our business so that we could spend less time and produce more substantial profits? Yes, of course it would.

This means that we should be able to examine the results we get with each action we take in a way that would allow us to eliminate extraneous efforts and enhance those efforts which bring superior payouts. When you think about it in this way, learning how to manage your time is like adding zeroes to your bank account simply by learning how to focus on your plans, choose the correct priorities, and then perform in a way that leaves nothing to chance or happenstance.

Once you discover the 20% of what you are doing that brings the 80% of your profits (the goal of having a business), you can increase doing those things and phase out the other 80% that brings in so much less profit. How much more time, then, would you have? And how much more profit?

Over time you will find that it becomes much easier to follow the three Ps (Plan, Prioritize, and Perform) simply because you will have more experience with implementing this concept. What you want to avoid at all costs is the dreaded fourth P – Procrastination! Procrastinating becomes a habit that rears its ugly head just at the moments when you are on a roll and picking up great momentum with whatever you are working on. That happened to Connie on Tuesday, just as this book was almost complete.

Connie had worked hard over the long holiday weekend, and found herself still tired when she woke up around five-thirty on Tuesday morning. She let her dogs out – she has lots of little dogs! – and had one split second in which to decide her next move. Instead of looking at her To-Do list and making a few notes before going out for her morning walk, she checked her email. This was a huge mistake. Because many people were gone for the holiday weekend and had now returned, she found herself inundated with messages that needed her attention. Her focus was drifting away from working on this book, in which case you might not be reading it right now.

Procrastination was slowly but surely taking over as she mentally slipped away from her original priority and now entertained the idea of putting that off for the time being to work on something else. Thinking back to the Time Management Matrix, this activity of personally answering these emails fell into the second quadrant, Important – Not Urgent, which is the most important quadrant to focus on as an entrepreneur. She froze in her chair as her mind raced about, neurons dancing and synapses crackling. Her fingers, just the index fingers because she only types with those two, hovered just atop the keyboard waiting for further instructions from above.

She closed her eyes and breathed deeply for half a minute, and then opened her eyes and, as Geoff often instructs, stepped away from her computer. She left the house and walked for thirty minutes, enjoying the fresh air and feeling the morning sun on her face and arms. When she returned from her walk she was ready for her day, and went upstairs to answer some emails. On that morning she had wrestled procrastination to the ground, knowing that this vile creature will darken her doorway again in the future unless she stays on top of the situation. It took Connie a couple of years of practiced implementation to get to this point in her life, but she now sees the value of utilizing the strategies we are sharing here with you in her own life and business.

What about the other things that need to be done, or at least at this point seem like they need to be done? There is a very powerful word that makes many entrepreneurs shudder. Hearing it makes them think they are giving up control of their business, or worse, their life. The opposite, of course, is true, but this reaction is an emotional one, not a logical one.

That word is "delegate". It is a lynchpin to any time management system. In the next section we will delve deeply into delegating, but know that, until you realize its power, you will be, to some degree, managed by time rather than managing it. You will be doing things that need to be done, but that aren't bringing you any closer to your stated goal or mission. Turn the page, then (or have your assistant turn it for you...) to start looking at this dreaded concept.

Do You Have To Do All Your Tasks? Doing Vs. Getting Done – Delegating

"If you want to improve how you manage time, stop doing what doesn't need to be done."
~Peter Drucker

You may be experiencing overwhelm in several areas of your life. If this describes you and your situation, simply slow down and do things in slow motion until you can sort it all out. You do not want to reach a crisis point before you do anything to remedy your situation. This happened to Connie while she was teaching and working in real estate at the same time. The seventy-hour weeks finally took their toll on her and she found herself too exhausted to carry on. She took a few sick days to sort things out and felt that her life was back in control enough for her to keep going. That was in 2000, and shortly thereafter she suffered a serious injury after falling at work. Looking back, she now says that taking a few sick days was just putting a band-aid on a much bigger issue that had to be dealt with at some point in time. The day she fell from the sink she was standing on in the back of her classroom to put up a bulletin board that was due at the end of the afternoon was the day everything, literally, came tumbling down around her.

The result of this event was that she was out of work for over five months, collecting disability checks instead of paychecks after back-to-back surgeries, and not able to work in real estate at all during that time. Her life turned upside down over the next couple of months, and financially she was going further and further downhill. She went through all of her savings during that those months, even though she put herself on a strict budget and did not live beyond her means.

While this was a humbling experience, it also made her face her circumstances head on. She was at a crossroads in her life where she was ready to change and just needed help knowing which way to turn. It was time for her to get her priorities in order once again and to reach out to others to help her through this tumultuous time. It took a full year for her to recover physically. She ended up in a physical therapy program that lasted from seven each morning until five in the afternoon. She did not miss a day in nineteen weeks at this rehabilitation facility and was not able to do any other work during this entire time. It would take her another year after that to recover financially, and the emotional healing was just getting off the ground as she made the decision to leave teaching as soon as she could figure out what to do next.

Most breakdowns, where people stop functioning and require professional help, can be linked back to issues with time management, efficiency, and productivity. As a classroom teacher Connie experienced quite a few families reaching the breaking point because years of disorganization and chaos had finally taken their toll. If you feel that this describes you then you must stop reading now and seek out expert guidance. However, if you are at the point where you still have control over your life and just need to be realigned, then this is exactly the right place for you. After what happened to Connie in 2000, she stopped to smell the roses and made a plan that would lead to her completely changing her life five years later. Sometimes we just need a catalyst to move us from where we are to closer to where we would like to be in our life.

Think about how you organize your daily life. Are you asking for help, support, and cooperation from those around you? Others want to help, but can only do so if they know what you need. Speak up for yourself and let the people in your life be of assistance. This is called delegating, and works in every aspect of your life.

Connie learned how to delegate during her second year as a teacher. She was sweeping and dusting the classroom after school while several of the students worked on their homework or went to the computer. She had just emptied out the waste basket when one of her students, Claire, said to her,

"Mrs. Green, why don't you let us help you after school?"

She smiled and said, "You don't need to help me. I'd much rather see you visiting with your friends and working on your school projects."

These were sixth graders, and she was concerned that they might not have the skills and study habits they needed to go on to junior high the next year.

Claire came over to her desk and sat down in the chair next to hers. She quietly explained that she and the others, both boys and girls, were used to helping at home. She gave Connie a detailed report of what she was capable of doing and how much it would mean to them if they could help keep the room clean and tidy. Then she stood up, looked Connie square in the eye, and said something Connie will never, ever forget.

"And we can do it better than you can, Mrs. Green, if you don't mind me saying so."

Claire was right! She had years of experience doing the exact things Connie needed done in the classroom.

Connie handed her the broom and the dust cloth and both of their lives changed forever.

An eleven year old girl had taught her how to delegate authority over tasks and projects that she was not very good at and did not enjoy doing. Learn to accept wisdom from wherever it appears and to not question the source.

It isn't clear why delegating authority is so difficult for many of us, but it is the single biggest reason why entrepreneurs never reach their financial goals. We wouldn't dream of doing everything around our house, such as mowing the lawn, changing the oil in the car, replacing the roof, installing a new dishwasher, or adding an extra bedroom, yet we feel as if we must be personally involved with every aspect of our business.

This often comes from a need to have control over our lives, especially if we come from a background where we had very little control or say so over what we did every day. The idea of giving up the control we now have can paralyze even the strongest-willed entrepreneurs.

The best way to move past this is to give up control of an activity you do not know how to do or do not like to do. You can also think of this as allowing people who play at the things we struggle with do what they do best, and let them do it for us.

The other thought, one Geoff has had, is that no one else can do it as well as he can. No one will have the same passion or attention to detail. But when you look more closely, some of the tasks that could be delegated will be done, as in the case in Connie's classroom, by someone who knows more about it and actually has more of a passion for it than you do!

It was simple for Connie to start with graphics and web design because she often describes herself as being 'graphics challenged'. When she came online at the end of 2005 she saw that she would need to be able to put up websites that had an aesthetic appeal to the people she was trying to reach. She found someone who loved designing sites and asked her to do some work for her. This person had the passion for that task that Connie lacked.

And because Connie was unable to do this for herself, she didn't even think of it as delegating, or outsourcing, as this is more commonly referred to in business. Over time she began to ease up control of many of the other activities and tasks in her business, such as submitting her articles to the article directories, answering customer support questions, and distributing content all over the Internet, and her bottom line increased very quickly and steadily as she did so.

She explains this by saying that she is only good at a few things, which include writing and creating content, speaking and presenting at live events, and creating online courses and teaching others how to build a business. By focusing in these areas and spending all of her time in the planning, prioritizing, and performing of these specific activities, she has elevated her status to that of a specialist.

And the other activities and tasks, those things that need to be done but are getting in your way and holding you back from moving toward your goals, are done by someone who wants to do them and is actually very good at them. Remember the 80/20 rule? Connie now focuses on the 20% that brings in the 80%. She delegates the rest.

There are also tasks that don't require any particular skill, that anyone with a fairly decent work ethic and a basic intelligence can be taught to do. You shouldn't be doing these tasks in your business. There is a phrase that has rattled around the business world for many years. Doing these things is not the 'highest and best use' of your time. This is also a phrase used in real estate to describe a piece of land that has not been improved with buildings that take it to its highest and best use, such as a piece of property adjacent to the downtown area of a city that still has a small home on it and nothing more.

Yes, if you love doing one or two of these tasks, go ahead, don't be a slave to this. But simple repetitive tasks can be very easily and inexpensively outsourced. You have just managed your time, not by managing your tasks, but by giving them away. You have instantly freed up your time to focus on the things that will make you money and will move you toward your goals and you have helped someone earn their living, perhaps even helped them start their own business by supporting entrepreneurs with this one simple but important task.

ACTION STEPS:

Look at tasks you do that get in the way of moving forward

Look at tasks you do that you could teach someone else to do just as easily

Delegate at least one of those tasks. Once you have done it once, you will start to see the power and will do it more often

Yes, But Which One Will You Actually Do?

"Schedule your life and defend it the way you would an important business meeting."
~*Tim Ferriss*

The very best time management strategies are the ones you will actually do. It's like anything else in life in that the methods and techniques will only work if you actively implement them.

You know yourself. If making detailed lists doesn't work for you, don't make detailed lists. This book isn't about making lists. Once you have a notion of what you really want to accomplish, the lists can take care of themselves. If you are someone who loves making lists, if for no other reason than you love crossing things off once they're done, make lists. Any of the specific ideas in this book are for your support, none of them are rules. Try them, use what works. What works for *you*. If timeboxing works for you, use it. Neither of us use the Pomodoro Technique® but both of us know it can be very powerful for some people so we included it. If you are one of those, use it. If not, put it aside.

Do the ones you will actually do. Good intentions to do it like Connie and Geoff do will get you exactly nowhere. "Well, at least I tried" won't help you manage your time or make you more productive. In fact, remove the word 'try' from your vocabulary altogether, for if you try to do something it is almost certain that it will never actually happen.

The main thing we want to stress, if it hasn't already become clear, is that you must have an idea where you are headed before you can get anywhere. Once you know that, the specific ways of getting there will become clear.

Do not be too hard on yourself if you find that you're still struggling after implementing some of the techniques and methods we have discussed here, remember that you are a dynamic being, constantly in the process of becoming the person you want to become. This takes time! Connie is known to tell people that it took her fifty years to learn how to live the life she now has; up until that time she was struggling to figure it all out, and for the rest of her life she will be refining what she's figured out and implemented up until this point. Geoff often says that everything he has ever done, every success, every failure, every accomplishment and every mistake, has helped him to become who he is today.

None of this is magic. It is all very practical. The way to manage your time is to first know what you want to accomplish, then to do what become obvious in order to accomplish that.

We recommend that you make a study of time management, productivity, and increased efficiency as it relates to your life and business. Read as much as you can, make a plan for yourself that you will follow, and then rework the plan to better suit your lifestyle. This is a process that will take some time, so celebrate your victories no matter how small they might be.

For example, if you are able to save ten minutes each morning by altering your routine, good for you! If you achieve greater results in one small aspect of your business by delegating just one small piece of it to someone else, hooray for you! Soon you will be taking a different path through the grocery store, shopping at a different store, or perhaps having someone else do this shopping for you. It's all about the choices you make to change your life one step at a time.

Section V:
Time Management and Productivity

*"Productivity is never an accident. It is always
the result of a commitment to excellence,
intelligent planning, and focused effort."*
~Paul J. Meyer

We have gotten great feedback about this book and a few days ago, Connie called Geoff and asked if it might be time to turn it into a physical book. We had both thought that might be the eventual plan when we started on it late last year, so Geoff enthusiastically agreed. First, though, we decided to go through it to see if there was anything we could elaborate on. Connie suggested that we delve more into the idea of productivity in terms of time management.

There is a fellow in Australia named Darren Ward who says that you can't actually manage time, that no matter what you do, it will tick away at its own pace. He says that what you can manage is what you accomplish in the time you have. This is the essence of productivity. For this section of the book, we are going to ask each other questions about what productivity means to us and for us.

Geoff: Connie, earlier in the book, you talked about how you lived paycheck-to-paycheck when you were a teacher, and how your money usually ran out before the next paycheck, but that there was nothing you could do about that, since you were already doing everything you could. How has your idea of productivity evolved since then?

Connie: I haven't thought about those days for quite a long time, Geoff, but I'm glad you've brought it up here. During those years, when I was struggling to balance my life in regards to family, health, finances, and two careers, it seemed like I was spinning my wheels and not being very productive in any of these areas.

It was all I could do each day to wade through the tasks I needed to complete in order to leave my house before six in the morning, do everything that had to be done in my classroom once I arrived at my school, go on to my real estate appointments after school, and then get back home and deal with my family before going to sleep in anticipation of doing it all again the following day. It was exhausting, to say the least.

The reality was that my productivity was at a very high level because I was managing my time so well. It just didn't feel that way because I wanted so much to be doing something else in my life at that time. I was caught up in what is referred to as the *momentum of mediocrity*, treading water but never quite making it out of the deep end of the pool.

The situation I am describing here happens to many of us, especially if we are doing tedious work that lacks the ability to spark our creative flow and doesn't pay very well. It's up to each of us to remove ourselves from the situation as quickly and as gracefully as possible to make room for whatever is to come in our life. I think of this as our unalienable right to seek our destiny.

This is the definition I share with my coaching students:

Proactive, Consistent Actions + Managed Time = Productivity

Geoff: It's fascinating to me that you say you were living "at a very high level of productivity and managing your time well" during this frantic time in your life. I know many of us have often found ourselves in circumstances where we are doing so much, feeling like we are using every available moment, and yet it seems nothing is progressing, nothing is moving forward at all.

When I was in college, I worked in the cafeteria for breakfast, lunch and dinner (and at special events such as when it was rented out for banquets), had a full load of classes, rehearsed in plays most evenings and found time to do my homework.

After college, I often held two jobs and still somehow found time to do "extracurricular" stuff like writing, working on plays, etc. (Of course, housework rarely seemed part of the bargain...) Even with all of this, the feeling I have is that I wasn't being "productive". Looking at your example, I suspect it was because I didn't have any real plan or idea of where I was going, just a vague, general notion.

I think there are many who find themselves in this state, working very hard, but going pretty much nowhere. I'm reminded of the Red Queen in Alice in Wonderland who said, "Now, here, you see, it takes all the running you can do, to keep in the same place. If you want to get somewhere else, you must run at least twice as fast as that!" We feel like the only way to move forward is to do more, to "run twice as fast as that", and we feel like there isn't any more we can fit into the mix so we stay in the same place.

Given this, do you have any thoughts or suggestions about how we can, as you say, "remove ourselves from the situation as quickly and as gracefully as possible..."?

Connie: Removing yourself from the situation only applies to the tedious and mundane, and to situations where we have outgrown our usefulness, *not* to activities and tasks that we actually want to achieve. If that is the case, simply complete what you originally agreed to, like I did when I worked in the classroom through the end of the school year in June, and then move on quietly to the next phase of your life.

What I am hearing you describe, Geoff, fits in exactly with what I have come to call the '3 Ps of Super Productivity™'.

In order to be overly, or 'super' productive I believe that we must have at least one of the following active in what we are striving to achieve:

- Passion/Purpose – When we are passionate about an activity it will not only go quickly, it will also make our heart sing.
- Prime Time – Activities that are worked on during the hours that we are the most alert, focused, and engaged will always produce optimal results.
- Project-Based – Working on a project, whether it's by ourselves or with a team, brings out the best in all of us. This leads to a feeling of pride in a job well done.

As you are describing your job as a cafeteria worker during college, I am envisioning a team of strong young students, excited to be spending that time together each day. I imagine you, Geoff, as the one bringing humor and laughter to the work, creating contests to see who could fill the salt and pepper shakers the fastest and daring the others to set the tables in a unique way, perhaps with a salad fork replacing a soup spoon! I picture you as a leader who never saw that job as a menial one.

And knowing you as I do, I'll bet you were much more engaged during the dinner hour than earlier in the day, because your 'prime time' hours are much later in the evening.

When you talk about having time to write and participate in acting and producing plays, I hear and feel the passion coming through your words. That was your reward for doing the hard work during the days. Your work in the theatre is an excellent example of a 'project-based' activity, where you feed off the energy and excitement of your group members as you accomplish your goal of taking the play from inception to production.

It's the ideas that are generated during our best hours of each day (prime time), based on our passions and purpose for living our lives (passion/purpose), that lead to the fulfillment of our specific goals (project-based).

I have been known to write for hours on end when I am passionate about the project I am working on. A recent example of this was when legendary marketer Marlon Sanders asked me to create a bonus for his new product.

When I first started working on this bonus report it was during a week where I had so much to do and was feeling the stress from having been ill for several days and then traveling to another state to speak at an event. The result was that I chose a topic I was not passionate about, worked on it during non prime time hours when I was tired and at an energy 'low', and I was not discussing it with my Mastermind group, my entrepreneur friends, or my list, to get the team support I needed.

After speaking with Marlon (a true pioneer and genius in the online world) at length on the phone, he gave me an idea that inspired me to write a bonus report that I couldn't wait to begin working on. I was in the airport waiting for my flight home from the event where I had been speaking while he and I were on the phone, and I began taking notes before my flight ever took off.

I made some more notes during the flight, but waited until early the following morning (my prime time hours) to actually do the writing. Within about four hours I had written almost three thousand words on a topic I'm extremely passionate about, and then sent it off to him to add to his site as a bonus.

The next step was to share what I had accomplished with my community on social media, to my list, and with my circle of entrepreneur friends. I was floating on a cloud for the next couple of days because of what I had been able to accomplish after being inspired in that way.

Find inspiration anywhere you can, and then take action in a focused and productive way.

Geoff, I have seen you inspired by hearing certain speakers present at live events, by a book you were reading, and by conversations you've had with me or others. I have then witnessed you becoming super productive in a way that is achieved by few men, all because you have allowed yourself to expand in to these '3 Ps of Super Productivity™'.

So, let's expand our definition of Productivity from...

Proactive, Consistent Actions + Managed Time = Productivity

to...

Passionate, Purposeful, Project-based, Consistent Actions performed during our Prime Time = Super Productivity

Now that we have discussed this topic in some greater detail, I have a question for you:

Geoff, when you have been super productive in your business during this past couple of years, can you describe the feeling it gives you both during and after you have accomplished your goals?

Geoff: That's an interesting question and actually has several different answers. I'll start with the "after". I always have a sense of joy and contentment when I have accomplished something I set out to do. That's easy to answer and I suspect most people feel that way. However, when setting out to accomplish something, there are different experiences depending on what's going on.

When what I am attempting to accomplish is something I know I can do, that I know is fairly easy for me, whether I have a passion for it or not, the feeling I have when doing it is of an easy flow. I can easily slip into what people have often called "the zone" with such tasks and projects. What that feels like for me is that the rest of the world sort of disappears and all that is present is the task at hand. Often, when in this state, I have no sense of the passage of time and sort of "wake up" at the end being surprised that so much time has gone by.

That isn't how it always feels, of course. When the project is something I'm not sure I can accomplish, that I don't know if I have the skills or experience for, that enviable "zone" is far away. With those projects (and there have seemed a lot of them in the last few years) I am almost hyper-aware of the passage of time. I often feel like I'm working against time to get them done, as if I had some massive deadline, or, if you want to get mythological, the sword of Damocles hanging in the air above me, just waiting for the chance to drop.

Once these projects have been accomplished there is an added feeling of satisfaction, of course. I have an odd and slightly embarrassing habit of wanting to go back over them again and again, partly to admire them, but partly to actually see and acknowledge what I've accomplished. (This can be with projects as diverse as having written a piece that I didn't think I was knowledgeable enough or skilled enough to do, or something as mundane as a thorough house cleaning.) I will usually indulge myself in this habit for a short time, but then force myself to put this project aside and move on to the next one, or I would be fearful of transforming from Damocles into Narcissus, staring at my own reflection for eternity at the expense of everything else.

Then there are those times I'm working on something that starts out being one like the latter, where I am conscious of every twist and turn I must take and somehow in the process, fall into that "zone" where I wake up at the end having accomplished it almost automatically. These are rare, though.

One of the ways you mentioned to be more productive (and that we've touched upon earlier in this book) is to find those things that must be done but that we either aren't good at or don't necessarily like to do. What many of us don't quite realize until we've done it a few times is that delegating, or giving those tasks away to others, is a fairly high form of productivity. They are still being done, but we are freed up to do the things we love, are good at and that will make a bigger difference in our own lives, our businesses and the lives of those around us. As much as I am gratified by being able to accomplish new things, it might be better to forego that feeling, let someone else accomplish that task, and only keep for myself the things that I know I'm really good at.

You have had a much longer experience of both delegating and accomplishing things that move you forward and help you and your business grow. What is that experience like for you?

Connie: As has been the case many times throughout our relationship, I am finding myself once again needing to 'Google' for the references you make! This time it's to find out more about the "sword of Damocles". Ah, now I see what you mean.

I can totally relate to what you are saying in regards to getting into "the zone" and immersing myself in my work. I can become so engrossed that I am completely and totally oblivious to the sights and sounds around me. Dogs barking incessantly, phones ringing, and people talking remain outside of my realm of consciousness when I "zone out". This is a glorious state, and one that we can especially benefit from as entrepreneurs.

Also, I understand your habit of 'wanting to go back over them again and again, partly to admire them, but partly to actually see and acknowledge what I've accomplished' when it comes to completing a task you have undertaken and achieved. Perhaps this is our attempt to recreate the experience so that it becomes deeply ingrained in our subconscious mind.

It's so interesting how we create these situations for ourselves where we are racing the clock, looking over our shoulder, and forcing ourselves to complete a certain task by a specific date and time. I see this as our subconscious mind's way of pulling us back into the time in our past where we had a boss or a supervisor who had so much say over our day to day life.

While I was teaching it was the school's principal who imposed these walls around my creativity. While working in real estate it was the client or the lender urging me forward while they cracked the whip at my heels. Actually, truth be told, the way I was feeling during these years of my life was simply me allowing others to make me feel a certain way. Once I let go of the anger surrounding my relationships with these authority figures in my working life, I was able to reframe it as them urging me to do specific tasks in a specific way in order to reach my full potential.

I visualized the principal, Mrs. Kravitz, as a wise and thoughtful soul who had my best interest at heart. My reframe included her always looking out for me by pushing me, ever so gently at first and then in a more forceful manner to achieve more in my career as an educator. This was quite a stretch from how I felt for many years when she was upsetting me almost every day for the six years I worked at that particular school.

When I was first working online and building my business I was embarrassed to admit the fact that I had worked for others until the age of fifty. But the online world is primarily non-judgmental, so I finally opened up and discussed my work history with the people who were attracted to learning from me. I shared how I felt as an employee for the public school district and as an independent contractor during my years as a real estate broker and appraiser, and how it all changed once I left that life behind and became the mistress of my domain.

As an entrepreneur we are freed of this bondage and must remind ourselves regularly of this freedom. My focus each day is to spend time doing what I love, which is writing, reading, learning, and creating, and then delegating and outsourcing everything else to people who are far more skilled than I am. These activities include setting up websites, rewriting private label rights content, spending time on the social media sites, and setting up my teleseminars, webinars, podcasts, and interviews.

I have long believed that we must not engage in the activities we do not truly enjoy because we are then taking that away from the person who does. Imagine someone taking on the tasks they dislike or have difficulty with, when these are ones you love to do, and not giving you the opportunity to do it for them? It would not feel right for either of you. Yet that's exactly what we are doing when we spend our precious time doing things that do not suit us.

Over time your preferences will change, so that something you once loved to do (in my case it was bookkeeping and preparing my income taxes) becomes something you have no desire to ever do again (the people who now handle this for me are computational wizards who make it all seem like child's play from my perspective).

Finally, let's discuss the level of enthusiasm necessary to achieve maximum and optimal productivity. This will vary from project to project as you move forward with your business. If you are not as passionate about one project over another it does not in any way diminish what you accomplish. For example, Geoff, as we finalize this last section of this book on time management strategies for entrepreneurs, we are not quite as excited and enthusiastic as we were when we wrote the original manuscript several months ago. This only means that we are both deeply involved with other projects at this time and is in no way a reflection on our commitment to excellence with this final addition to the book.

However, there is a direct correlation between your speed of implementation and your income, so do not allow anyone or anything to get in your way when you have a new idea.

Geoff, say something about the amount of time it now takes for you to go from creative thinking and initial idea to completed project when it comes to one of your digital information products or online courses.

Geoff: I think that question goes right to the heart of why some people are more productive than others. There are people who, as soon as an idea occurs to them, they put things into place to make that idea happen. Then there are those who ponder the idea, discount the idea, set the idea aside, or even think, "yes, that's a good one", then either wait for inspiration as to how to do it, or simply don't start because they don't immediately know how to accomplish it.

I think the ability to immediately put things into practice is one that can be learned. I've seen and heard about people who do it all the time, but it isn't necessarily an innate gift. It's one which must be developed. For me, there are ideas I get that seem grand ones, but also seem like they will take me off the path to what it is that I want to accomplish in the bigger scheme of things. It doesn't take a long time for me to determine if something will take me toward that or away from that. If it will take me away, I put it aside. If it seems it will take me toward my ultimate goal, I'll want to start jotting down ideas about it right away and move forward as quickly as possible.

However, often, I will come up with a good idea, jot notes, begin planning, and then set it aside for any of a number of reasons. When I do this, rekindling it can be difficult. This is where working with other people can become invaluable. When you have told someone you are going to create something and they are waiting for it, even if the initial passion or purpose has begun to face, that promise, that desire on another person's part can be something to anchor to, something you can attach yourself to in order to put into place what needs to be there to get the project done.

As an example, I have a book that I've been working on for quite some time. It's about the myths that artists cling to that keep them from producing their art. I have most, if not all, of the content done, but the shape of it was wrong, somehow. It wasn't coming together at all. But I have an accountability partner and I'd told her that I was working on it and wanted to get a draft of it done by a certain time. When I realized that I needed to go back and rework it, it would have been very easy to just let it go. However, her commitment to me getting it done re-infects me and this project is now taking shape rather nicely.

What is your experience of that, the time from the creative idea, through the planning to the completed project?

Connie: I'll get to my answer to that question, but first I'll say that I agree completely with you that in order to be optimally, or 'super' productive we must choose projects that will move us closer to our 'Big Picture' goals. I teach that for every action you take throughout your day, whether it is related to our business, our health, our relationships, or to something else we must always ask the question "Will this action move me closer to or further away from my goal?" we must continue doing what will move us closer and immediately cease all actions that are moving us further away. Delegating and outsourcing can be invaluable here.

It is also true that being able to take immediate action on an idea is a learnable skill. Practice makes perfect with this, so look for opportunities to stretch yourself in this area.

It was when I was first working with a Mentor and his Mastermind group five years ago that I encountered the problem of not being able to implement new ideas immediately. We would brainstorm ideas for each other for many hours over a three day period in the group meetings, and then each member received an mp3 recording of their session to listen to later on. This was convenient for everyone, as it's difficult to take notes while you're front and center and the group is hurling ideas at you at the speed of sound!

The problem was that I would listen to the replay a week or so later, take a few notes on what they had suggested, and then go about my daily routine. If they had recommended something small, like changing my picture on a profile page or changing a headline on a sales letter I would do that right away. The deeper, more detailed changes would take me weeks, or even months, and sometimes I would not take action on them at all. It was as if I was paralyzed into inaction. Looking back, I'm not sure what was stopping me from taking immediate action, but perhaps it was my lack of confidence in my abilities or a lack of being totally committed to my business as an online entrepreneur. In any case, I lost much time due to this and I have to take 100% responsibility for the outcome during that period of time.

I then made it my goal to implement what I had learned and had been told by people I trusted, within seven days. This wasn't easy, but running a successful business requires that you stretch outside of your comfort zone on a daily basis.

The results were quite impressive; each time I took action I could see the fruits of my labor within days or weeks. Also, as I became more skilled in working faster, smarter, and more diligently, my mind was opened to more possibilities.

You may have heard a saying that goes something like 'fail fast, fail often, and fail forward'. This is what I strive to achieve every day in my business, as well as in my personal life. This is not an audition, this is real life and it's time for our most effective performance each and every day. We don't need to ask permission or give a thought to what anyone else would think. It's time for massive action!

Geoff, I'd like to wax philosophical now. We in the Western world tend to be 'in our heads' a lot, and perhaps that is part of the reason we do not accomplish our goals in a straightforward way as many Eastern cultures seem to be able to do. How do you get inspired to be productive, and how can you and I inspire others to do the same?

Geoff: What a wonderful question. I don't often talk about that part of things because it can scare people away, but I believe we are 100% responsible for our own inspiration. We think of it as some muse, something separate from us, whispering in our ear or prodding us to do something, but it is actually our subconscious mind, which has been churning and mixing all the information we have fed it, feeding that information back to us in new and exciting ways.

There are lots of different ways to be responsible for our own inspiration, and I could go on about it for hundreds of pages (in fact, I have gone on about it for hundreds of pages in other forums than this) but there are very practical things we can do every day to jump-start ourselves, to focus in so we can accomplish great things.

Sometimes, all it takes is focus, but most of us in the Western world don't quite know how to direct our own focus. One of the many exercises I like to do (and I call it an "exercise" on purpose. It may seem like I'm advocating meditation, and, although meditation can be very powerful, this is not that. It is something far less esoteric and far more grounded in practical reality) is to start the day with working my imagination. How I structure it is to open a blank document on the computer, take a brief moment to get an idea, then start typing the details of some wonderful future.

I fill in details for three or four paragraphs, never stopping to edit, never worrying about if any of it is possible. It's just a dream, but it's a focused one. I usually find myself beginning to smile a few sentences in, however. Once I'm done, I sit for a very brief moment, "recalling" that future that I just made up, then see what's on the schedule and get to work.

This exercise does several things. It is extremely pleasant, for one, and so it is easy to do. It also gets our mind really focused. Once we are in a focused state, it's very easy to continue to focus on the next task and the next. This way, our day starts both pleasantly and with direction.

If that one doesn't appeal to you, there are many audios out there that are designed to help you focus. I'm not talking about hypnosis or, again, meditation, I'm simply talking about things that bring the mind in from the frantic wandering we are used to in our busy lives. (I've even created some of these audios myself and people seem to respond very well to them.) Something that takes ten minutes or less can change our entire day.

You may have noticed that I keep insisting it isn't meditation. Meditation can be, as I said, a very powerful thing and science has shown us that it can even alter our thought patterns. However, meditation has connotations of magic. Also, true meditation, like the Yogis can do, takes years to perfect and we in the Western world simply don't have those years. It also takes a long time to meditate and we usually don't have several hours at the start of the day to give over to that. Having something quick simple to use is all we really need.

So when I find myself "uninspired" to move forward (and, yes, it still happens to me), I find one of the many exercises I've found or created over the years to assist me to get focused and present to what needs to be done, spend five or ten minutes with that, then get to work.

(In our book, "The Inner Game of Internet Marketing", I go into greater detail about several of these, by the way.)

Connie, I also know that you have techniques that you use that may not seem at first glance to be part of "time management" or "productivity" but that help you get done what you need to do. Can you elaborate on any of them?

Connie: I'd be happy to, Geoff. Thank you for sharing your experiences with inspiration in regards to focus and productivity. And as far as pursuing a muse, I am reminded of the Albert Brooks film *The Muse* where a screenwriter seeks the help of a woman who appears to be a daughter of Zeus, in order to rekindle his writing career. But I digress.

I like to plan my life at least a quarter ahead. By this I mean that I keep a calendar of what I will be working on for the next three months or more. This includes personal goals, such as a trip or special event with family or friends, as well as business planning, which includes writing, product creation, affiliate promotions, and live events.

When someone asks me if I am available next month on the first Thursday at noon, it is easy to see if I already have something scheduled. This may seem like a simple thing, but I have much more free time when I schedule it all. Just this week I was able to attend the Cowboy Festival with some friends and neighbors, simply because I had added it to my calendar almost two months ago. Everything moves smoothly and effortlessly when you do this on a regular basis.

Earlier in the book, I talked about the 'rocks, pebbles, sand' where the philosophy professor poured ever smaller sizes of rocks and pebbles into a jar, finishing with sand to show that, if you focus first on the small stuff, there is no room for the stuff that is actually important.   You must take care of the important things, such as taking care of your health, finding the right people to share your life with, and building a profitable business with residual income if you are to get to a place in your life where you can put this model into place. I have many students who want to jump directly to the lifestyle without laying the foundation. This leads to disappointment, struggle, and disillusionment with the process I am describing here. Instead, focus on your 'rocks' each and every day.

Here are three steps to get started with moving ahead productively:

1. Commit to being productive every single day
2. Automate, templatize, and systemize everything you do more than once
3. Delegate and outsource what others can do better and faster than you can

Following these three steps will enable you to accomplish more in less time, will allow you to have more free time to spend as you like, and will raise your self-esteem as you gain a deeper appreciation of what you are doing in your business and personal life. One of my favorite quotes applies here:

"Do for a year what other won't, then live the rest of your life the way others can't".

Geoff, what else would you like to add?

Geoff: We've talked about productivity from several different viewpoints, now. The idea that we can be "productive" (i.e. very busy) and still not get anything done if we aren't focused on what we want to accomplish in our lives is very profound. We also touched a bit on how we can inspire ourselves (the only way we really *can* be inspired) to be more productive. These both point to the "inner" side of things. Then there are the practical steps to take to actually get things done. These are from the "outer" side of things. You need both, I think, to be really productive.

Connie: Yes, we must have both the 'inner' and the 'outer' to be balanced in our work and in our personal lives. I'd like to leave our readers with a short checklist for what they can put into place right now to be as productive as possible.

- Determine when your 'prime time' hours are and plan to work on your most important projects during that time each day. Because my best time is early in the morning, I guard that time by going to sleep by eleven or so most nights, and not scheduling anything else before nine or ten in the morning so I can leisurely work on my writing.
- Make sure to have what I refer to as 'quiet time' for at least thirty minutes once a day. Geoff talked about

meditation, but this time can also be used to sit in quiet contemplation while you daydream about the solutions to your problems and the ways to achieve your goals.

- Find a Mentor or accountability partner to connect with at least twice a week. This person will help you to stay focused on what is important to you right now, over the next thirty days, and a year or two into the future.

- Stretch yourself every day. I'm not talking about physically, but that's an excellent idea as well to get the blood flowing to your brain. I'm referring to what is sometimes called 'thinking outside the box'. I find that by challenging myself to learn and take action on something new on a regular basis, my life and my business have greatly benefitted. You will still feel the resistance, but knowing that everything you need to know is a learnable skill will make it possible for you to attain your goals. In recent times this has included learning some Finnish (not so easy!), line dancing, and cooking some of my favorite dishes.

- Write down exactly what you want to achieve, when you want to achieve it by, and when you actually do achieve it. This has now been scientifically proven to work. Simply by taking the time and making the effort to put your ideas and goals into writing changes the way your mind will synthesize it into more concrete terms.

We hope you have benefitted from this section of the book, and hope that you will now feel empowered to move forward productively. Best of success with everything you set out to achieve in your life and in your business. Let us know how we can be of service to you.

Connie's Time Management Worksheet

Since we can't do anything to gain more time in our lives, managing the time we do have is the only solution.

The key to this is finding out how you are spending your time right now and to then modify and adjust your actions to make yourself more productive and stress-free.

First, keep a record of how you are currently spending your time each day. Do this for a typical workday and also for a day off. Make a chart that shows each hour between the time you wake up and the time you go to sleep. That will give you an excellent indication of times throughout your day where you may be wasting time, or at least not making the best of it in a particular situation.

For example, I have a meeting I attend every month that is held at a location more than thirty miles from my house. I live in southern California, so I never know just how long it will take me to get there because of the traffic. To ensure that I was never late, I was leaving my house ninety minutes before the meeting was to begin. Sometimes I would arrive just in time to get in and take my seat, whereas on other occasions I would be there almost an hour early. This was quite frustrating and stressful.

Now I always leave my house ninety minutes before the meeting will begin, but the difference is that I bring my Kindle and a small notebook with me so that I have something to work on while I am waiting in my car. Over the past year I have probably created about two extra full workdays out of the time I would have spent just sitting and waiting for the meeting to get started without having any materials with me to work on. I actually look forward to the wait these days because it is so relaxing to read my Kindle from the comfort of my car, and to make notes and do some writing on one of my projects.

Next, make a list of the activities you are doing on a regular basis that could be done by someone else. I used to dread waiting in line at the post office. I would justify this wait by checking my email on my phone or reading through my mail during this time, but it was a weekly time waster more than anything. I found someone to help me with some other household errands, and she is now the person who goes to the post office once a week for me. By delegating this activity, I freed up six hours a month. It also feels good to be employing someone who needs to make some extra money, so it's a win-win situation. If you do not need to do it personally, delegate the activity to someone else.

Finally, schedule some time just for yourself each day. I found that by doing this I was much more productive throughout the remainder of the day. The best time management tips sometimes include things that actually take up more of our time. I like to sit quietly outside in my yard from about nine-thirty until ten each morning. By this time I have been working for about three hours or so, so this is my time to think and enjoy nature.

Resources:

Massive Productivity Timer:
http://MassiveProductivity.com

Time Management and Productivity Book List:
http://GeoffHoff.info/timemanagementlist

About the Authors

Connie Ragen Green is a former classroom teacher and real estate appraiser who left it all behind to become an online entrepreneur in 2005. She now speaks internationally on the topics of getting started with an online business and how to make huge profits with a tiny list. She also teaches new online entrepreneurs how to get started with their own successful business. Connie resides in southern California and is also an active volunteer and supporter of organizations such as Rotary, Elk's, and Zonta. Visit her site to learn more at http://HugeProfitsTinyList.com.

Geoff Hoff, known as The Creativity Expert, has been a creative writer, an actor, an acting teacher, a standup comic and a popular blogger. He studies and writes about the process of creativity and the process of marketing and teaches creative writing and marketing courses on the Internet. He lives in Los Angeles. To find out more, please visit his website at http://GeoffHoff.com

www.ingramcontent.com/pod-product-compliance
Lightning Source LLC
LaVergne TN
LVHW052302060326
832902LV00021B/3676